Resolving Inner Conflict

The Most Effective, Permanent Solution To Finally Overcome Inner Conflict For Life

Pam Johnson

Table of Contents

Introduction

Chapter 1 - Your Inner Demon

Chapter 2 - The Pain You Locked Away

Chapter 3 - Redeeming Your Stolen Identity

Conclusion

Introduction

Have you ever caught yourself arguing with your own thoughts? Have you ever been caught between a tug-of-war of two opposing yet equally desirable choices? But you know in yourself that you can only choose one. If these scenarios frequently happen in your life, then maybe you are having problems with inner conflicts. Whether you are aware of it or not, inner conflicts can cause difficult circumstances. You can actually avoid these conflicts if you know how to handle inner conflicts well.

I want to thank you and congratulate you for purchasing the book, *"Resolving Inner Conflict: The Most Effective Permanent Solution to Finally Overcome Inner Conflict for Life"*.

This book provides the knowledge you need in resolving the unpredictability of your inner conflicts. The awareness this book brings will light up the dark world of your inner battles. It is divided into three chapters which explain the nature of inner conflict and the relation of emotions with your inner conflicts. You will also learn applicable and comprehensive solutions to permanently triumph inner conflicts.

This book also provides strategies and practical steps that you can easily apply. Find out how to win a battle within by being fully equipped with knowledge, power and perseverance.

Thanks again for purchasing this book, I hope you enjoy it!

"And even though today I might feel run over and feel heavy-hearted for a few people that I love, there is a promise that tomorrow I will be stronger, more patient and better refined person. We are to be brought through fire, not left in it."

—Hayley Williams, Paramore

Chapter 1 - Your Inner Demon

"I'm free, finally free," Lacey mutters to herself as she read the thick journal she'd written last year. As she read each entry, she remembered how awful she felt at the time she wrote them. She recalled each tug-of-war of emotions that sucked every ounce of energy from her body. Her miseries were obvious in her messy handwriting. Every erasure shows how much she tried to gather the perfect words to describe how she felt.

Each journal entry portrays the inner conflicts she struggled with; conflicts that people around her said she could suppress by fighting back. So she fought her feeling, but she found out that she only hurt herself more.

Although the emotions from her past came back to in waves, she knew that she is now different from who she was yesterday. She is now living in the "promise of better tomorrow" she chose to believe a year ago.

The change didn't come easy, but it did make life easier for her. Her renewed perspective towards inner conflicts enabled her to experience life with peace, hope and joy. Her knowledge about inner conflicts freed her from unnecessary sentiments, decisions and idleness. It's not really about creating a new version of herself. It's about getting rid of an inner demon that has been bullying her mentally and emotionally for years.

Maybe in some way, you also experienced having conflicts with yourself. Perhaps, two opposing thoughts gave you many a sleepless night, or maybe even made you doubt your future. In the midst of those dilemmas you're always left questioning how much effort you must cxcrt to push that pessimism away. You tried everything to dissolve all the negative thoughts lingering in your head, but positive thinking seems insufficient.

Well, you don't have to endure life that way anymore. This book will show you how untrue the criticisms of your inner demon are. Hopefully, this book hopes to enlighten you how worthy you are of a life full of delight. It may not be a life completely free of negativity but a life that has full control of inner critics. This is the end of the mental and emotional torture that inner conflicts brought to your life.

WHAT IS AN INNER CONFLICT?

An inner conflict is the clashing of two opposite, yet equally desirable, interests within a person.

An inner conflict is a moral, mental or emotional hurdle that you struggle within yourself. It usually happens every time you are in situations that involve doing what you think you need to do versus what you want to do. Most of the time, external factors, such as the environment, influence the situation.

For example, an inner conflict happens when you crave for a triple layered burger with bacon while you're on a strict diet. Its mouth-watering smell tries to shut that inner voice in you, alarming you of the bad effects it might cause to your health. Then you start to argue with yourself whether you should buy a burger or not. However, if you didn't go to your favorite fast-food restaurant in the first place then none of this would have happened. Well, there are cases of inner conflicts that are more serious, but this is the simplest way to illustrate how an inner conflict happens.

Inner conflicts are actually healthy. It is part of the human nature. What's unhealthy is when you remain clueless of what inner conflicts are and what they can do. Such lack of knowledge may lead to unwise decisions and unanticipated emotional breakdowns. The longer the person is oblivious to this fact, the closer he is at walking the path towards the destructive road of inner conflicts.

DESTRUCTIVE INNER CONFLICTS

Multiple ignored inner conflicts can become a monster. It can eat up your sanity and steal your joy. As you continually fear the negativity it gives, the stronger it gets. As a result, your behavior will grow into something too difficult to handle. You might find it difficult to pull yourself together.

This is what actually happens inside the minds of suicidal people. Their ignorance of inner conflicts and their lack of knowledge about it only brought them misery. That's why telling them to "be positive" or "you don't have to feel this way" doesn't really work at all. The grip of their inner bully has become too strong, so much so that they start thinking that the only way to escape their inner demons is through the sweet release of death.

HEALTH CHECK

In a hospital, the doctor will examine you first before providing the necessary treatment. Similarly, you should also examine yourself before dealing with your inner conflicts.

Here is a short list of the symptoms of inner conflicts. This will help you weigh how destructive your inner conflicts have grown. Being acquainted with these behavior patterns will help you trace the root of your inner dilemmas. It will make you understand how to face your inner demon as well. Just say if each statement below is true for you or not. It will be much better if you note them down in a diary or journal for future use.

- Other people's opinions usually influence mine.

- I'm always having a hard time making decisions.

- I feel doubtful to the decisions I already made.

- Most of my relationships are dysfunctional, rampant with conflicts and have no sense of harmony.

- I always have sudden unnecessary and unpredictable change of mood.

- I always distract myself whenever I'm faced with an inner conflict (like getting drunk, taking drugs, excessive work, being busy etc.).

- I always seek support from others because I feel like I am incapable of handling them.

- I feel impulsive, anxious and depressed whenever I'm faced with challenges.

How many of these statements are true for you? How does it make you think and feel? Accepting these brutal truths about yourself may give you a sense of discomfort. But keep in mind that this is just going to be temporary. The awareness you have right now is the start of the dissolution of your inner conflicts. Make this as a stepping stone on knocking your inner bully down.

There's no need for turning back now. You are walking on the right track.

Chapter 2 - The Pain You Locked Away

People have a natural psychological defense mechanism. They feed themselves lies to protect themselves from the harsh reality. It's like little white lies that you tell people you care for so they won't feel offended or hurt. In other words, people tend to curl up inside their comfort zones instead of facing intense emotional encounters of truth.

While this defense mechanism seems like shock absorbers of pain, the solution of the real problem [inner conflict] remains nonexistent. In fact, it can be a self-deception to those people afraid of change and confrontations. And that is when the formation of small blocks of fear and anxiety begins to take place.

Do you know Elsa from Disney's Frozen? Do you know how the conflict in that movie started? Because Elsa wanted to protect her sister Anna from her powers, she locked herself up in her room and hid from all the people around her. She actually believed it's her only choice. Now, that's a great example of a psychological defense mechanism. That movie clearly portrayed how destructive an inner conflict can be, how it can distress everyone around you and how running away can never be the solution.

Although Elsa is only a fictional character, her role excellently portrayed nonfictional struggles that many people face today. Her story also showed the possibility to break the ice that inner conflicts created in your heart. However, it's going to be more than letting go.

BENEATH CHRONIC EMOTIONAL EXPERIENCES

People are not as free as they think they are. Democracy isn't enough to guarantee someone's freedom. That is because political freedom is different from psychological freedom. Psychological freedom is intangible yet present. That is where you need to free yourself. However, it can only happen through understanding depth psychology.

Depth psychology is the process of uncovering the roots of negative emotions. Those are usually the cause of emotional suffering, self-defeat and self-sabotage. It is like undergoing psychoanalysis but in a lighter level. You can do this by yourself. However, it is better if you involve at least one person to help you figure out things. Having another person help you will make it easier for you to find your blind spots and tell you about the things you missed about yourself.

Levels of Negative Emotions

In identifying the negative emotions you should deal with, you should familiarize yourself with these two levels of emotions: the symptoms and the sources of symptoms. The symptoms are usually the results of an unresolved inner conflict. This level of negative emotions includes boredom, loneliness, worry, anxiety, stress, depression, self-pity, insomnia, cynicism, feelings of being trapped, chronic patterns of failure, addictive behaviors, psychosomatic ills, and so on.

These symptoms are just the results of deeper emotions from unresolved issues including feelings of being deprived, rejected, betrayed, refused, manipulated, criticized, abandoned, helpless, and unloved.

People are likely to hold on to these emotions. Unintentionally, they tend to replay and recycle these negative until it has dominated their thoughts and decisions already.

It may be a bit discouraging to get to know these negative emotions. But then again, your awareness about them is the key to set free the pain you have locked away for years.

THE FOUR CORE EMOTIONS

It's obviously easier to take medications for your insomnia, depression, or whatever ails you, but if you think about it, these solutions are just short-term at best. The reason why these pills can't provide long-term effects is because most of them are just treating the symptoms. For you to eliminate the symptoms, you should tear down the roots of the problem first.

So this part of this chapter will let you see the four core emotions that stems out all the other destructive negative emotions and behavior. These emotions have the potential to destroy you and drive out of your most important relationships. So focusing on these four emotions instead of the long list mentioned above, will allow you to know where all your inner conflicts are coming from. Tracking down these inside killers is your next big step towards the door of permanent freedom.

The Silent Killer

Guilt is the feeling of "owing" someone, especially if you know you did something wrong to that person. That inner disappointment shakes you emotionally. For instance, you promised a friend that you'll attend her birthday party, but certain things happened and you weren't able to come. Because you didn't fulfill your promise, you are now full of guilt. This feeling of guilt makes you feel that you're irresponsible, incapable of fulfilling promises, and unworthy of other people's trust and friendship. Your guilt makes you feel indebted to the person you've wronged, and it makes you do anything to make it up to that person; that's the trap of guilt.

No one can turn back time no matter how hard he or she tries. So the guilty person feels trapped and helpless to make it up with the offended party. Consequently, the guilty person tends to think that he must do something else to cover up, or at least lessen the damage he has done.

An example of this is a man who had cheated on his wife. The guilt of his wrongdoing makes him assume that the solution is to make it up to his wife. Maybe he'll try making more effort, giving gifts, etc. However, that's not going to heal the pain at all. That failure will cause more and more inner conflicts between the man and wife until their marriage is at the brink of failing.

Guilt silently kills your relationships by making you believe that things are undoable as long as you can provide an alternative to your misbehavior. Therefore, as guilt continues to control your external life, your inner conflicts become harder to conquer.

The Explosive Killer

Anger arises when you feel as if someone did something wrong to you. It makes you believe that you don't deserve the things you got. It is anger itself that branches out feelings of bitterness and resentment. Or worse, it results to violence, too.

While bitterness helps him absorb the pain he received, what the angry person didn't know is that, it doesn't take his resentments away. It doesn't cool down his anger either. Wallowing in bitterness actually worsens the rage forming in his heart. As a result, it prohibits him to gain inner peace and experience happiness—something that he doesn't deserve to feel either.

There are signs that point out the presence of anger in your mind: you are quite irritable, inefficiency in accomplishing duties, bitterness and the like. If you get overpowered with anger, it will lessen the chance of winning your inner battle. This is because anger clouds up your ability to understand. If you're having a difficult time understanding things, the harder it will be for you to handle your inner conflicts.

The Discontented Duos

By definition, greed means the need to possess more things than necessary. The word "enough" is not in the greedy person's vocabulary. These kinds of people find value and satisfaction in material things.

These emotions result to damaging behavior such as lust or hunger for things like money, sex, and power. This feeling makes them believe that hoarding possessions, titles and achievements will give them a sense of triumph and relief. But what they don't notice is the poison that lives within those feeling of triumph and relief.

As the seeds of greed grow bigger, it is inevitable to feel envious as well. As soon as these joint emotions break into your thoughts, you will start feeling resentment towards other people, and you will find yourself constantly criticizing them. These emotions might even set off depression.

Working hard for material possessions is a general human nature. People are natural hunter-gatherers, they survive by making sure they have what they desire and need. Satisfying your needs is part of what life is all about, but you should not let negative emotions like greed, envy, guilt, and anger dictate your decisions.

It may make you pay the price of destroyed relationship, restlessness, anxiety and discontentment. If negative emotions like these continue to dwell inside of you, your inner critic can use these emotions to have more control of you.

THE POWER OF EMOTIONS

Emotions are powerful, which is why advertising companies use them to improve their marketing techniques. They create ads that yield these four basic forms of emotions to hook their consumers to buy their product.

An example is a single working mom who has little time to cook for her children, but sees an ad about ABC canned goods that supposedly is as nutritious as home-cooked meals. The ad brought out feelings of guilt in the single mother; it makes her think that she isn't paying enough attention to the nutrition of her children because of work so she buys ABC canned goods. Now, if advertising companies were able to figure out how to use human emotions for their benefit then so can you.

The Purpose of Emotions

Unfortunately, there are more negative emotions than positive ones. What this is means is that you will get nowhere by ignoring your negative emotions and clinging onto the positive ones. Actually, there are no "good" or "bad" emotions, it's all about how you express and deal with them. The best thing that you can do is to look for the purpose of the emotion and try to understand why you are feeling that way instead of drowning yourself in the sensations they emit. You should treat these sensations as "signals" that will warn you about your emotions.

Chapter 3 - Redeeming Your Stolen Identity

This chapter will provide you with tips and practical steps on how you can overcome your inner conflicts.

RECOGNIZE SIGNIFICANT EMOTIONAL EXPERIENCES

Living a life full of emotions is part of being human; it's what makes us different from the other living creatures on the planet. You will not enjoy a movie if it doesn't stir up your emotions, and music seems lifeless if the composer did not put all of his emotions into writing the piece. There is beauty in emotions, they are not just there to make you feel bad, and this is what you need to realize.

It is part of being a human to experience a life full of emotions. It is a gift that makes human unique among all the living things on earth. A great movie can never be satisfying if it did not succeed in steering your emotions. The emotions attached to music are what make music immortally remarkable to the hearts of people. The point is, there is beauty in each emotion and that is what you need to recognize.

The problem is that most people do not welcome, or even accept the fact that they will experience negative emotions sometimes. They believe that only positive emotions are the ones that are beneficial, but that is not how emotions work.

There is no such thing as desirable or undesirable emotions. Each emotion plays an important part for your inner growth. Emotions only become detrimental or destructive if you ignore and refuse to deal with their purposes.

For instance, a woman wants to feel loved and she expects her partner to only make her experience positive emotions, but that is not how relationships work at all. Being loved means there will always be times of conflicts, misunderstandings, corrections, and a slew of other emotions. When the woman starts feeling these negative emotions, since she does not recognize their purpose, she starts acting negatively as well. However, if she recognized that these negative emotions are parts of being in a relationship, she might not tend to wallow in bitterness, depression or frustration.

The first step to overcome inner conflicts is to recognize the purpose of your emotions. It's okay to feel bad. It's only a matter of accepting and understanding that those are part of your inner growth; and the more you grow inside, you will become stronger emotionally.

LEARN TO IDENTIFY AND RESOLVE CONFLICTS

The previous chapters of this book taught you how and why inner conflicts happen. Now, it will be much easier for you to identify the conflicts that make you feel uncomfortable. Since you now know how to recognize significant emotional experiences, negative emotions will have less control on how you see and deal with conflicts.

In identifying conflicts, it is important to understand both sides, especially if it is serious. For instance, you want to make new friends, but a voice inside you makes you fearful of rejection. You have made your reasons for wanting to make new friends clear, and you need to determine why you are so afraid of rejection. Identify the main root of that fear. Are there unresolved negative emotions from your past? Are there things you should settle in the present?

Remember that inner conflicts have causes and effects. If the effect of a conflict to you is negative, there must be a negative cause as well. Only by resolving the cause of your negative emotions will you resolve the effect. Once you identify the cause, do not hesitate to think up of solutions.

PRACTICE POSITIVE HABITS

One of the strongest forces that pull you down into the labyrinth of inner conflicts is the existence of negative emotions. Previously, it was discussed how the four core emotions can cause great damage in you and the surrounding people. While positive talks can't simply make these emotions go away, positive habits do. Here are five positive habits that you must practice to break the chains of the strongholds of your negative emotions.

You are strongly encouraged to practice these habits as much as possible. If you desire immediate and effective results, you must commit yourself to the process. If you don't then all your efforts might go to waste.

Confession

Confessing is the habit that breaks the chains of guilt. When you confess with the person you have wronged with, it will provide healing in the both parties.

But the most important confession you should do is the confession with yourself.

What actually makes the feeling of guilt worse are the lies people play in their minds. They believe that as long as they can provide an alternative to what they have done it will negate its effects. So first, you need to be honest with yourself before you can do the same to others. It may not eliminate their anger, but it will surely lessen it. They might even trust you more for being honest.

Forgiveness

The vicious cycle of anger goes like this: feel better, release it and feel bitter again. As you can see, simply releasing anger doesn't provide any cure. If you really want to get rid of anger, learn to forgive. Whether the offender asks for forgiveness or not, learn to forgive them. Don't wait for a "feeling of forgiving" because forgiveness is not a feeling at all. It's something that you have to do willingly. The moment you made the choice to forgive, you are freeing yourself from all the resentments you are carrying for so long.

Generosity

The habit that beats the power of greed is generous giving. Remember that greedy people do not feel content so being generous is the best way to break the chains of greed. Giving allows you to experience a change of heart since your act of generosity makes someone else happy. So give until you start feeling a change come over you and this will spill over into your lifestyle.

Celebration

Among all the emotions, envy is the most cancerous since it makes you compare yourself with others. You might even start comparing yourself to your past self. It makes you empty, trapped and restless. The perfect way to overcome envy is to practice celebrating small accomplishments. It doesn't matter if it's yours or of the people around you. Celebrating each progress you make keeps you driven and happy at the same time. On the other hand, celebrating the achievements of others will help prevent envy from taking root in your heart.

Love

Love is the strongest above all emotions. If it seems hard to forgive, remember to love. Remember how undeserving you are of the bags of grudges that keep you from experiencing happiness. Remember how other people chose to love you in spite of your faults and imperfection. Remember to love others in the same way.

Wake up to each morning with thoughts of love and wear that feeling the whole day. If love motivates you, it will be easier to confess, forgive, give and celebrate. Let all things in your world— inside and outside—revolve around love.

STAND HIGHER THAN YOUR INNER CRITIC

Positive self-talk are common nowadays. Though it's useful for many people, positive self-talks might not be as effective if you are in an argument with your inner critic a.k.a. inner bully.

Imagine a school bully giving a smaller kid a hard time, but then the small kid tells him, "Why are you being so mean to me. Did I do anything to offend you?" How do you think the bully would react? Would he stop mistreating his victim or would it make him want to beat up the smaller kid even more? Your inner bully responds in the same way a real bully does. It's probably because you often act passively against your inner bully. To explain this further, below is a dramatization of a conversation between a person's inner critic and inner passivity.

Inner Critic: You messed up another friendship again?!? When will you stop being a burden to everybody?

Inner Passivity: I know I failed in many things, but I always try to do my best to be a good friend.

Inner Critic: No, you don't deserve to have friends at all.

Inner Passivity: I did my best to love them. I gave everything I can for my friends. Maybe they just don't see it.

Inner Critic: No, they just don't care at all. Are you kidding me? Do you think people really appreciate you? They're just being nice. Their reputation matters, not yours.

Inner Passivity: You're right. Maybe I'm better off alone.

How do you think this person can love himself if he permits this inner bully to belittle him? His passive behavior is actually the thing that limps him emotionally. If he didn't allow this inner conversation go that way, the inner critic will go away. The best solution is to stand higher than your inner critic does.

Don't put him in a spot where he can hold you accountable. Don't let him dictate whether your actions are wrong or not. You are not his slave; you can do much better. Just think of your inner bully as a tool to help you grow. Don't let your bully become a burden that you have to shoulder.

SECURE YOUR IDENTITY

Most people think that their behavior defines their identity. However, the truth is that it also includes your thought patterns.

Your past actions do not define your identity. It shouldn't define your present or future. In dealing with conflicts, it is essential that you secure your identity. Knowing who you are makes you want to act more naturally, which actually makes handling inner conflicts easier. It's not about finding your true self; it's about embracing your true self.

GIVE IMPORTANCE TO THE RIGHT THINGS

There are five areas of your life that you should give great importance to when resolving inner conflicts and they are your values, decision, passion, goals and motives. Giving clarity to your personal views towards these essential elements of your personality prevents massive inner conflicts from clouding your mind.

Draw the line between what you believe as wrong and right in every aspect of your life. It will be better if you have a strong basis about this, like theological, spiritual or philosophical foundations. Then align all your upcoming decisions with your values system. Next is to set goals driven by the appropriate passion that also supports your core values. Lastly, identify what keeps you motivated to pursue your goals and, again, make sure that they align with your values.

RECORD EVERY CHAPTER OF YOUR JOURNEY

Your journey is going to be tough. Engaging in an emotional inner battle can prevent you from thinking rationally. So keeping a journal is important. Keeping records of your progress will allow you to think through the how's and why's that you go through every day, which will make it easier for you to come up with solutions. It can also be a permanent reminder of what you've gone through and how you rose up from those challenges. Your journal can be a source of inspiration for your future self and the people under your influence.

Conclusion

"What the caterpillar calls the end of the world, the master calls a butterfly"
—Richard Bach

Thank you again for purchasing this book!

I hope this book was able to help you to understand the best solution in overcoming your inner conflicts. I hope someday in the future, you'll be like Lacy (in the first chapter) whose life has been transformed by choosing to look at inner conflicts as stepping stone in growing into someone better. I hope as you look back to this day that you have decided to apply everything that you learned in this book, you'll smile with regrets left behind—together with the negativity you have thrown away.

Just always remember that even dark times make you feel helpless and paralyzed, you have the choice whether you believe that feeling or not. You have a choice to stand up and keep chasing the life you deserve: meaningful, vibrant and full of hope. You have a choice to make. Now is the perfect time to do that.

Finally, if you enjoyed this book, then I'd like to ask you for a favor, would you be kind enough to leave a review for this book on Amazon? It'd be greatly appreciated!

Thank you and good luck!